SUCCESS IN BEAUTY

THE SECRETS TO CONFIDENTLY
FOLLOWING YOUR DREAMS EFFORTLESSLY

COMPILED BY CHARLOTTE HOWARD

#1 International Best Selling Author | Beauty Transformational Life Coach

Charlotte Howard - Heart Centered Women Publishing 108 Flintlock Lane

Summerville, SC/USA 29486
www.heartcenteredwomenpublishing.com
charlotte@thehairartistassociation.org

Book Cover ©2015 Charlotte Howard - Heart Centered Women Publishing

Book Layout ©2015 Charlotte Howard - Heart Centered Women Publishing

Ordering Information:

Quantity sales. Special discounts are available on quantity purchases by corporations, associations, and others. For details, contact the "Special Sales Department" at the address above.

Success In Beauty: The Secrets To Confidently Following Your Dreams Effortlessly Compiled by Charlotte Howard. —2nd ed.

ISBN-13: 978-0692550809

ASIN: 0692550801

Foreword

When asked by my women clients how I got to where I am at today in my life and business, I said "You have to make up your mind, what you want. You have to make up your mind, what you are prepared to give up getting it.

You have to set your priorities, and then take massive action." Coming from a single mom who started working as a corporate beauty salon hair stylist, and was diagnosed with carpal tunnel syndrome, I ended up creating what I want in life by becoming an entrepreneurial woman. These words are something to be seriously taken note of.

When I asked the beautiful and authentic women in Success In Beauty: The Secrets To Confidently Following Your Dreams Effortlessly what did they do to confidently follow their dreams, I was very surprised at what they shared with me. So much that I was destined to get this message out to all the women in the world.

"Success In Beauty: The Secrets To Confidently Following Your Dreams Effortlessly" is an extraordinary road map that is designed to provide you with the direction, purpose and drive that you are looking for.

Each of the chapters in Success In Beauty: The Secrets To Confidently Following Your Dreams Effortlessly includes hidden secrets never shared by other women that will walk you through the process of creating what you want from your life and then, how you are going to get it.

This book will enable you to stop procrastinating along in life – instead you will discover what your life is all about and how you can go about to confidently follow your dreams as a woman.

"Success In Beauty: The Secrets To Confidently Following Your Dreams Effortlessly" will be your very own life map of where you are now to where you want to be. You will soon rediscover those lost ambitions, those dreams and passions that had fallen by the wayside. This is the time to start a fresh new journey.

So start right now!

With love, Charlotte Howard

#1 International Best Selling Author, Publisher and Beauty Transformational Life Coach http://CharlotteHowardInfo.com

Preface

"Success In Beauty: The Secrets To Confidently Following Your Dreams Effortlessly" will help you break through all barriers and fixed notions you have about confidently following your dreams and passions in life and guide you on how to move forward with creating a life you want.

Confident women are successful. They stick it out until they get what they want. This is because they confidently believe in their goals and their own ability.

If you are reading this now, you are aware that a lack of confidence has seriously held you back in achieving your most important goals in your life. It is time you put an end to you lack of self-belief.

You don't want to be shy and quiet when the women in the world around you are confident and full of life, do you? So, fight the fear and get what you want – FOLLOW YOUR DREAMS WITH CONFIDENCE!

The Persevering kind!! To your success, Charlotte Howard

#1 International Best Selling Author, Publisher and Beauty Transformational Life Coach http://CharlotteHowardInfo.com

Table of Contents

Angela James

Angela James is a visionary change agent, mentor, facilitator, speaker, intuitive consultant, energy healer, writer, singer, dancer, visual artist, teacher, community and educational activist and mother. Angela merges a variety of highly effective facilitation techniques with her highly intuitive abilities and offers workshops, individualized intensives, private one-on-one sessions, retreats, group coaching programs and classes. She is a self-admitted, but recovering overachiever who has worked as a consultant for Fortune 500 companies for nearly 30 years. Angela has longed to trade in her corporate (not so 9-5) life to help others discover their magnificence through their unique skills, gifts and talents.

Release Your Brilliance Out of the Shadows and Into the Light

As a very young child, I felt very different from everyone around me and was very comfortable about it until I realized that in our society, being different was not considered such a good thing. I came to the conclusion that I needed to conform to be like everyone else because in the end, the odd man out is never wins. This was the beginning of me dimming my light and hiding in the shadows.

When I was young, I was an amazingly creative being. I was so intrigued by all art forms, dancing, singing, drawing, playing musical instruments, drawing, painting, poetry, sculpturing, sewing, cooking…etc. You name it, I did it and exceptionally well. Problem was my family brushed these my "gifts" of mine off. I remember really wanting to be a singer. I loved entertaining. I remember always having to perform for family and friends. Although I was the family entertainer, my family didn't give me encouragement to become a singer. Instead I was told that I needed to focus on a career that made me money, like being a doctor or a lawyer. Since I was really good in math and science, I was encouraged to be a doctor. I bought into the idea and at some point in time, being a doctor was indoctrinated in my brain! So, when people asked me what I wanted to be when I grew up, I would always say that I wanted to be a pediatrician and a singer… I wasn't sure what my plan was for doing this……. All I knew was there was something in me that didn't want to let the concept of being a singer go, so I became a closet artist and eventually lost the desire because my family praised my receiving good grades in school more than my excelling in "the arts".

Fast forward to college years……. I became a Pre-Med student and solely focused on taking classes relative to my major. I took dance and gymnastics classes for the purposes of keeping in shape more so than the fun of it. My senior year was a big

8

turning point for me. My father and mother shared my college expenses. My father paid my tuition and my mother and stepfather paid my room, board and incidentals.

During my senior year, my mother and stepfather got a divorce, and I received no more financial support from them. I had to find a job to pay for the things they covered. I applied to medical schools but didn't get past the application process because one of my summer school transcripts from a different school didn't arrive on time plus I really didn't know how I was going to pay for it since I was depending on my mother and stepfather to foot the bill as they promised me they would. My future as I had once envisioned it was over. I didn't have a Plan B or a short-term plan for after graduation, so I continued to work the job I had to get as a senior. Then as luck would have it, I ended up getting pregnant and getting married, in that order. Going to medical school was so not in the plan now.

Fast forward to now……. For so long I was living the SUPERWOMAN lifestyle, going through the motions of being everything and everywhere and working hard for everyone but ME! My marriage didn't work out, but that's a whole story within itself. I became a single mom of 3 and felt I had to do what I had to do to keep my children living the same lifestyle they had in a 2-parent household and to feel secure and loved. Again, I didn't have a Plan B, but knew I had to just do what I had to do to keep my household in flow. I had what most people would consider a "good career." But this career path never offered me fulfillment. It just paid the bills and allowed me to provide for my family. I have always felt something deep inside me that there had to be more for me in this lifetime, but I could never define what that "more" was.

I had forgotten what my hobbies were before I had a family. I had forgotten how to have fun. I had forgotten what brought ME joy and happiness. Since I wasn't doing what I THOUGHT I wanted to do when I grew up (which was to be a pediatrician), I really had no idea what to do anymore. I was in a total state of confusion. For so long I was living the life that everyone else expected me to live and didn't even know it....until the universe came by and smacked me in the face with a BIG TIME wake-up call!

Several years ago, I was diagnosed with an autoimmune disease called sarcoidosis, and there is no known cause or cure.

The disease affects people in different ways and can affect several of the systems in the body. For me it has affected the eyes, lungs, skin and heart. Steroids are used to help control symptoms, and after my initial treatment with steroids, I took a deep dive into a dark space.

My body hurt and I was in a lot of pain. I went from being this highly active person to a person who was always tired. I couldn't sleep at night because I had this never-ending cough. I was a hot mess, and I just didn't want to live anymore if I had to live like this.

I asked God to just take me away. But apparently God didn't listen. The steroids I was taking were making me gain weight, and boy oh boy did I gain…. not only that, I had to take other drugs just to counter the side-affects from the steroids.

I knew this was not the course for me. So, since God wasn't going let me leave, I knew I had to do something to get out of this space. I began studying different healing modalities. I began to tune into my body. I started paying more attention to my intuition and made better choices on my path to recovery. In the midst of my discoveries, I became more and more aware of my being and knew that the path that I was on was actually a part of my journey as well as what I needed to experience as a part of this journey.

After years of learning and experimenting, I have become a highly stimulated, very intuitive creative machine. I holistically healed myself. I have opened my creative juices and have written plays for elementary students, planned community festivals and health fairs, designed and made costumes, composed songs…....AND am singing again! I am being called to share my knowledge and gifts with the world and help others discover their magnificence through their unique skills, gifts and talents.

I truly believe that everyone is equipped to be the brilliant and magnificent being they came on this earth to be. I have organized a networking group for women so that they can get together and have fun while mixing in a little business! I wanted to create a container where women could get together and showcase their brilliance out of the shadows and into the light and do so in a fun, non-threating environment. I also have a coaching practice where I work with individuals to help them discover their magnificence.

Here's what I know. We dim our lights and hide in the shadows so others can't see us for various reasons. We carry memories in our subconscious which often becomes a part of what makes us afraid to express who we truly are. It is almost as if that which is contained in our subconscious minds becomes a part of our psyche and infuses itself into our being. This happened to me. I wasn't living. I was just existing. I had become numb to living in a state of joy and letting my light shine.

It took my getting ill to awaken me, and it took deliberate action for me to clear all the gunk in my mind, let go of the past and limitations I placed on myself so that I could live fully in the present. All of us have a unique mission on this earth. Not living out my mission caused me to be unhappy, feel unfulfilled, and hide in the shadows.

Living out my Plan B Life helped me to identify what makes me truly happy and put the steps in place to achieve this new vision I created to live a life filled with fun, possibilities and fulfillment. I now choose to live fully, unconditionally and unapologetically! I have embraced releasing my brilliance out of the shadows and into the light. Isn't it time for you to did the same?

The greatest discovery of all time is that a woman can change her future by simply changing her attitude. -Charlotte Howard

How Will You Confidently Follow Your Dreams Today?

_____
_____
_____
_____
_____
_____
_____
_____
_____
_____
_____
_____
_____
_____
_____
_____
_____
_____
_____
_____
_____
_____
_____
_____
_____

_____
_____
_____
_____
_____
_____
_____
_____
_____
_____
_____
_____
_____
_____
_____
_____
_____
_____
_____
_____
_____
_____
_____
_____
_____

Bonnie Bonadeo

Bonnie Bonadeo - Arakara LLC, The Beauty Agents Speaker –
Education Resource Company, Beauty Goorus Coaching &
Consulting, and Co-founder of Naked Audience Productions. Bonnie
has represented the beauty industry 25+ years by *Connecting People to
the Power of Beauty.* Her experience in the industry started as a stylist,
to managing salons, and working for some of the most notable
manufacturers and distributors to directing the industry's most
celebrated events. As a 2013 Enterprising Women and a certified
Emotional Intelligent Speaker, Bonnie specializes in leadership, public
speaking, sales and personal branding programs and classes and
authentically speaks on her struggles and successes as a leader and
entrepreneur to foster growth and awareness in others.

www.napevents.com
www.thebeautyagents.com
www.beautygoorus.com
https://www.facebook.com/bonnie.bonadeo
https://twitter.com/thebeautyagents
http://www.linkedin.com/in/bonniebonadeo/
https://www.youtube.com/user/thebeautyagents
http://www.pinterest.com/bbonadeo/
http://instagram.com/bonniebonadeo/#
http://www.twitter.com/naptraining
http://www.facebook.com/naptraining
www.bonniebonadeo.com

Pulling the Threads of Your Life Blanket... Are You Naked Under There?

I have always had this innate ability to connect with people, partially because I am not afraid to speak to strangers and partially because I am so curious for the answers that I am willing to ask the questions or share of myself to have others provide insight to me so I can ponder in what I don't know or have just learned. Either way I am not afraid to speak my truth as they say.

Others are sometimes offended by my openness, sometimes saying TMI Bonnie... Or they are just staring at me thinking "I have never asked myself that question or thought about it like that". In my ability to share of myself it at times unravels others but that is the trick to connection sharing of yourself, just be prepared for the consequences.

The consequences and how your good natured connection can be used against you.

Consequence 1: Most people don't want to be exposed, they like the blanket or veil they are hiding beneath, so there is a chance they will avoid connection as it uncovers a potential deep feeling or past experience in them. These are the **Naked Avoiders**

Consequence 2: Others will use your empathetic approach to dump and download on you and expect solutions, advice and problems solved from your curious and caring nature. These are the **Emotional Addicts**

Consequence 3: People will gravitate to you like butter crème frosting and look to you as a new, warmer and sweeter blanket to hide beneath. These are the **Enabled Junkies**

Connection Era. No matter what level of connection you may provide or hope to achieve with the avoider, addicts and junkies, they're out there. They will use you, abuse you and take from you until they blame you, judge you and leave you for making them feel as though they are a bad person.

We sometimes don't see ourselves in these areas and inevitably someone gets hurt or feels offended. It seems like read one of these stories on Facebook at least once a week.

Some dear friend or even best friend turns on you and speaks their truth and disappears in a wake of massive confusion, uncommunicated expectations and unresolved communication. Poof!

They are gone. You are left with what did I do, why would you say that to me, what happened that I don't understand, how can I apologize for something if I don't know what it is? What just happened

I want you to be present in this moment right now... It may have been something you did, but not to directly to them. It may have been something you said, or are doing, it may have been your own life hurts or inadequacies that you have expressed looking for a sympathetic ear and only to get backlash because while you are unraveling the threads of your life blanket, without knowing pulled at theirs too.

Connection for the most part is the most effective way to grow and prosper. Think about it, if you are isolated and not connecting with others then how you could prosper. There are many songs in the world about how we are all one and our innate need to connect with others, from a physiological stance to procreation to sharing common interests and hobbies, but how does that explain the intimate relationships we need with others past our procreating years, the ability to have a connection with a person in a truly intimate way, whether that is a friend, business or marriage relationship. As humans we are emotional beings the emotional connections we must have as individuals is critical to our survival and sustainability. This is no joke, you have heard of people in long time relationships once losing their partner end up dying from a broken heart. They see no reason to live without that connection and maybe feel too old or scared to establish new ones.

So what is going on in our high tech society when connections are happening a billion times a minute via the internet, social sites and more… and none of it is human connection? Is that still connection? The kind we need to survive or is it showcasing symptoms like a drug that we are becoming addicted to our phone and the internet. Human connection in its most authentic form would never be considered an addiction but instead true compassion and empathy for human kind. I see myself on the hot seat of feeling isolated, lonely or just bored and reach for my phone to connect instead of other alternatives like taking a walk, meditating, calling a friend or family member of just going to a place like Starbucks to be around people to feel and experience connection even if it starts out as false connection it leads to me feeling more connected. Are we addicted to the connection of our smart devises? Is this new kind of connection altering our ability to truly be present with others and be naked!

The Naked Truth….

Of course when I say naked it means uncovered from how the world may see us and allowing ourselves to be seen as we are in the world. It could also mean uninhibited or no fear to be truly authentic.

When we begin the journey of pulling at our threads of our life blanket… it automatically has others looking at theirs and even when your pulling on yours with someone that you have a true connection with could automatically begin pulling on theirs….not judgmental, or intentional but a true test of turning the mirror on themselves to see the thread unraveling and their life as well.

What better opportunity then to blame you for the unraveling of their life when all you were doing was working through your own unraveling sharing insights with determination to live more peacefully and with joy. True Joy, not just happiness as happiness which can be fleeting, external or materialistic but true joy that resonates inside of you because you have done the work, you are no longer afraid to pull the thread of your life blanket knowing that is may never stop unraveling and even if it does, guess what, you may no longer have a blanket all stitched together to protect you but you will have a big pile of thread that is your life…

Now I do not want you to think this big pile of thread is a mess that you have to stitch back together. Instead, I want you to see that when you don't have to keep protecting yourself you can live a more fulfilling and joyful life. Free of hiding, covering up, being armored. It may feel scary and cold when you first start unraveling, you may feel disoriented and disorganized, thinking I always do it this way and panic trying to stitch it together again, but it will never be the same once undone and this is transformation of self.

This is believing, behaving and bestowing as yourself as you are right now in the world, no hidden agenda, no fear, no real past showing up in your future because whatever is in your past has already happened and occurred so it no longer needs to keep hanging around like an old dingy blanket.

Now, even in reading the words I wrote in the last paragraph, I know that all sounds like whip cream with cherries on top and the pie in the sky approach, and there are probably thousands of books saying this same thing and if they didn't work before why would they work now.

Here is what I want you to know… as humans we will always come from our ego side and our Amygdala part of our brain is designed to protect us from danger harm and threat but what if most of the threat we are protecting ourselves from is not a real threat only perceived, what if our emotions of who we are in the world could heal and that we understood we are enough, what if we discovered we are our own worst enemy to making the changes in our lives that propel us because we are too afraid to unravel our life blanket.

What if we didn't ever change or pull the thread... what will our lives look like a year from now a decade from now...what will changed for the better... what experiences would we miss out on both happy and challenging and yet we could say we lived, we truly lived if we unraveled....with one pull that led to a life in motion until we were naked, naked of fear, of the unknown, of dying, of forgiving, of loving, of choosing, of believing in ourselves enough to say I am what I am and I am enough to walk, run or skip though my life naked.

Your new life it waiting so keeps pulling at the thread of your life blanket until you find yourself. Your true self....It's all about YOU connecting with YOU and then and only then can you connect with others!

Surround yourself with women who are going to lift you higher.-
Charlotte Howard

_____
_____
_____
_____
_____
_____
_____
_____
_____
_____
_____
_____
_____
_____
_____
_____
_____
_____
_____
_____
_____
_____
_____
_____

_____
_____
_____
_____
_____
_____
_____
_____
_____
_____
_____
_____
_____
_____
_____
_____
_____
_____
_____
_____
_____
_____
_____
_____
_____

Chandra Rohr-Chriswisser

Chandra Chriswisser is a very busy woman, balancing being a mother, wife, entrepreneur, educator, hairstylist and makeup artist who loves a good challenge. She believes in facing challenges and fears head on, getting them out of the way, and move forward to your dreams. Growing and evolving each year has been the key to her success. She is living her life her way, leading an amazing team, running a successful business, teaching other stylists to reach their full potential, and raising a family.

Learn more at: http://www.ohanasalonaz.com
https://twitter.com/ohanascottsdale
https://www.youtube.com/user/ChandraOhana
https://www.facebook.com/Ohana-an-Aveda-Concept-Salon-Spa-116553668431004/timeline

Have Courage and Keep Moving Forward

How much more could I possibly take? Throughout my life I have always managed to muster up the courage I needed to keep moving forward, but in 2010 I had a failing dream, a baby on the way, and my husband's job wasn't going well. The bills were rolling in and we could barely afford to pay for gas or food. I was trapped, drowning in this mess not knowing or seeing any way out.

I have had to overcome a lot of obstacles going back to my childhood. My parents both worked full time and even overtime trying to keep the family afloat. So I spent my days balancing school, homework and helping to raise my siblings. Even at a young age I was drawn to the beauty industry and would do makeovers on my family and friends.

I doubt my brothers appreciated this very much but it helped to light the spark for the passion I would have for this industry. When I was 14 I went to a salon, it was the first time I had been in a real salon. I watched this hairstylist working and she was beautiful; she had this amazing presence about her as she was talking and laughing with her client. When she was done with her client's hair I saw the client's eyes light up and you could tell she felt beautiful.

Before this moment I hadn't realized that this was something I could do for a career. I knew then that my dream was to become a hairstylist and I wanted to begin immediately. I was just starting high school and I was a good student but I just wasn't into it. I wanted to begin my career. I knew I still had to get a diploma so I transferred to an accelerated high school and was able to graduate at the age of 16.

I was living in Colorado and at the time most of the cosmetology schools I was finding were really cheesy, stereotypical beauty schools that smelled like perms and looked like the 80's threw up; that was not what I was looking for. I wanted a school that was chic and stylish, so I started looking elsewhere and found an Aveda school in Arizona so, despite my parents protest and concern of my departure after I graduated, I packed up my things and moved to Arizona.

I realized quickly that I had made the right decision. I felt like this was my world and I couldn't wait to get started on my own. Starting out in this industry at the age of seventeen was a challenge. I began working at a salon in Scottsdale where I assisted for two years before getting my own chair. Like all dreams, mine began to grow and evolve.

After working there for 10 years I felt that I had reached my full potential. I was a hair color educator for Aveda and booked solid with clients, but I wanted more. I wanted to open my own salon. I envisioned a place that was high-end but still comfortable. Where clients would love coming and leave them wanting to come back. I wanted a team of stylists that I could train to be the best and create a reputation for creating beautiful hair and making people feel good. I wanted to create a guest experience that would set us apart from any other salon in the industry.

In 2008 I opened `Ohana Salon and Spa with a colleague. We wanted our guests to feel like family and have a high quality experience. I thought with my professional experience in the industry I would be able to go into this new venture with the knowledge to get things going smoothly and growing quickly. I never imagined how different it would be running the business; dealing with employees, marketing, client complaints, trying to grow other people and handling the daily issues.

It wasn't like coming to work and getting to play with hair and makeup all day. I was way out of my league and it was much harder than I expected. I reevaluated and dove deep into meditation trying to determine if this was the right path for me. I came to the conclusion that it was, and if I gave up I would never forgive myself.

However, after a couple years we were struggling financially and having a hard time making ends meet. The spa brought its own challenges and was losing money monthly. This was how I ended up in my predicament in 2010. I had to stop taking a paycheck and start working for free. I was the top producer and I had to work just to keep the doors open. During this time I also became pregnant with my first child, and the timing couldn't have been worse.

At this point I was in so deep without taking a paycheck that I was behind on all my bills and barely making it. My husband and I had to file personal bankruptcy, which was a hard decision. I never thought that would be in my life plan, but I had no choice and it was the only way out.

After filing for bankruptcy I had to start all over again but at least I could breathe.

I had also given birth to a baby girl which was my saving grace at the time. She kept me grounded and gave me the purpose to keep going. I still believed in my dream and now I felt a boost to get back on track and be a role model for her. So I immersed myself in business books and started following entrepreneurs that I admired getting information on how to be successful. During this process I realized that I was loving the game of business just as much as doing hair and I got my 2nd wind to get the business going.

The next couple of years were spent working on a new business plan. In the midst of this my husband and I decided if we wanted another child this was the cut-off time to decide. We agreed that it was time and I became pregnant with our second child, a baby boy. With having two kids and a business, finding the right balance was a challenge. It took time but I was able to get a handle on it all. In 2015, I became the sole owner of `Ohana Salon.

I immediately closed the spa, which lifted a huge weight off my shoulders, and expanded the salon. I am continuing to perfect what we do to make our customer experience even better. After 7 years in business I finally feel like I have figured out the right formula for success that works for us. In business, you can never let yourself become stagnant. Watching the salon continue to evolve and change has been one of the most rewarding aspects of being an owner.

Don't lose sight of your dream always keep in mind that it's up to you. The way you react and handle things is what is going to keep you going. There were times that I felt like it would be much easier if I would just quit pushing myself and be happy with where I was currently at. But I knew if I did that it wouldn't be what I truly wanted. So many people get stuck in life and never finish getting to their dreams because they feel like its too hard, or someone made them feel like they couldn't do it.

You have to break through that and stick to your goal; if you fail it's because you let yourself. Don't live with regret and let the years go by constantly wondering what it would have been like if you'd kept going. Whatever happens, don't pull the victim card if something doesn't work.

Redirect and find another way, no one can take your dream away from you unless you let them. Dreams can change and take on a different angle.

For me, I didn't start out knowing that I wanted to be an entrepreneur; I evolved into that and my dream evolved. Always keep moving forward and be willing to change it up. Surround yourself with a good support system of family, friends and colleagues that are in your court cheering you on. I know this journey would have been so much harder for me if I did not have the constant support of my husband, family and friends to motivate me and keep me pushing forward.

The title of this book is "The Secrets to Confidently Following Your Dreams Effortlessly" but following your dreams is not without effort; the key is to make it look effortless. Doing this takes time, practice and the courage to keep going no matter what gets thrown at you. If I can do it, then I truly believe anyone can. You just have to be willing to try.

If you want to accomplish your goals in life as a woman, you have to work hard on yourself.-Charlotte Howard

How Will You Confidently Follow Your Dreams Today?

_____
_____
_____
_____
_____
_____
_____
_____
_____
_____
_____
_____
_____
_____
_____
_____
_____
_____
_____
_____
_____
_____
_____

How Will You Confidently Follow Your Dreams Today?

Charlotte Howard

Charlotte Howard is a world renowned beauty salon marketing expert, author, speaker and eCommerce leader. She trains and "MENTORS" families worldwide on how to create FULFILLMENT and HAPPINESS in their lives. As an elite 46x's international best selling publisher and award-winning hair artist, she uses inner and outer grandeur beauty strategies as a foundation for empowering families to create success in all areas of their lives. She has been featured on ABC News 4, Live 5 News and many other media outlets throughout the U.S and abroad.

Learn more at:

http://TheHairArtistAssociation.org

http://SuccessandBeauty.net

http://About.me/CharlotteHoward
http://HeartCenteredWomenPublishing.com

Achieving Anything Your Heart Desires

"Leave nothing for tomorrow which can be done today."-Abraham Lincoln

This must be a quote you have heard a hundred times before. There is of course a kind of simplicity in the way these nine words convey a simple message – don't put things off for later.

Are you one of those people who always put off things for later? Well, you are not alone. This is a problem that almost everyone goes through at least one time in their life.

At the age of 8 years old I lost my biological father in a very bad car accident. His funeral was on my birthday. Among the things that make individuals happy and pleased is the company of loved ones and friends. The emotional back up these individuals give you is priceless.

You probably don't enjoy being smothered by your family, but getting together for a cook out once in a while hearts up your happiness level. Having individuals around you that you love, trust, cherish and care for makes you feel that you're not alone.

This year when we had our cook outs it felt different because my biological fathers' brother passed away. It felt like my biological father dieing all over again. He use to take us to Disney world every year when we were younger and when we got older he joined us for cook outs every year he never put it off. He traveled all the way from New Jersey to see us and always had the latest and greatest movies and stories to share.

When it comes to opening your life up to others, you may feel a little hesitant. You may not want to open yourself up because you are uncomfortable with new people or you have mistrusted people in the past, but you need to find ways to overcome the issues and to allow yourself to open your heart to others.

You will find that sustaining and maintain friendships and relationships can be very hard, but they are also interesting and can be passionate. You never know what a relationship or friendship might bring you in the future, but one thing is for sure, you need to learn how to get over the past and live for the future.

My uncle tried to call me by phone a couple of days before he passed away but I missed his phone call. I said I will call him back later but it was too late when I called him back. That's why it's so important not to put things off if you can help it.

I didn't want to continue on with my businesses. In fact I took 3 weeks off to clear my head and to be there for my family. Even though I took time off my business still operated with my team. If I didn't have a team I would be out of business and would have worked for nothing.

Now look toward the ground and notice if there are any ropes holding you down, stopping you from being free to fly. In order to go on in your life, it is necessary to cut those ropes--to overcome not your fears of failure but your fears of success.

When it comes to your inner energy, you will find that you have all the strength within you to get up and achieve or seek out whatever it is that makes you happy. You should try to seek out a happy, healthy, and fulfilling life. When your time is up, you will want to be able to say that you've done it all, however, many people fear the end because of all that there is that they want to seek.

What is it that you wish to seek out? You need to be able to define what you want so that you can dig up all the energy inside yourself to help you achieve your goals. You should also try to realize what type of energy that you have and how to tap the energy out of you when you are trying to seek a goal.

First, would you say that you are normally an optimistic or pessimistic person when it comes to your overall attitude of your life? If you find yourself positive, then you should consider yourself fortunate to not let others drag you down. If you are negative then you need to find ways to turn your negative into a positive.

One way to convert your energy is to seek a massage therapist. That's right a massage therapist, especially one that specializes in Reiki massage. This is a type of massage that allows all your negative energy out and to fill you with hope, peace, and love. Not to mention it will help you with your goals in life.

You will find that when your energy has been cleansed, then you will be able to carry on with your life with all intentions of reaching for the stars. When you have positive energy you will find the strength to do anything, now all you have to do is use it.

How are you able to tap into your energy to help you deal with some of your goals and the obstacles that you need to pass? Well, the only way for you to use it is to realize that you have the power to do whatever it is your heart desires, and that you allow yourself to reach your goals.

For you to get the energy to meet a life-changing goal, you need to know that you are capable of doing it and you have to have passion. It is the passion that will make your goals obtainable. You need to want it so bad that you got to do it and if you want something that bad, there is nothing that will ever stop you from getting it. All you have to do is know what you want out of life. If you can define what it is that you want then you will be able to achieve all that you have set in mind.

Once you can define the goals and who you are, the picture will come in much clearer. You will notice that your goals will seem to become closer and you will be able to work your way up to some of the life goals that you have met. When you hit a rough spot you have two options; either push forward or quit.

Do you really want to quit, or do you want to see it through? If you have passion, your decision will be automatic. You will find a way to meet your goals and to have everything that you ever dreamed of come true. However, it is hard and you need to put a lot of effort forth. If it is something that you truly want then you will find a way to achieve it.

The best journey you can take is to confidently live the life of your dreams. -Charlotte Howard

How Will You Confidently Follow Your Dreams Today?

_____
_____
_____
_____
_____
_____
_____
_____
_____
_____
_____
_____
_____
_____
_____
_____
_____
_____
_____
_____
_____
_____
_____
_____

How Will You Confidently Follow Your Dreams Today?

Charlotte Howard

Charlotte Howard is a world renowned beauty salon marketing expert, author, speaker and eCommerce leader. She trains and "MENTORS" families worldwide on how to create FULFILLMENT and HAPPINESS in their lives. As an elite 46x's international best selling publisher and award-winning hair artist, she uses inner and outer grandeur beauty strategies as a foundation for empowering families to create success in all areas of their lives. She has been featured on ABC News 4, Live 5 News and many other media outlets throughout the U.S and abroad.

Learn more at:

http://TheHairArtistAssociation.org

http://SuccessandBeauty.net

http://About.me/CharlotteHoward
http://HeartCenteredWomenPublishing.com

Confidently Manifest Your Dream Business & Life

Have you ever wanted to accomplish something in your life or business, but you were unsure how to get started? Or maybe you set a goal and then couldn't figure out the right actions to take? Or you set the goal, started taking action – and nothing happened. No results – zip, nada, zero. I certainly have during my journey in life.

Sometimes goal-setting is like trying to find your way out of a very large (and very confusing) maze. You know where you are, and you know where you want to be, but the area between "here" and "there" is shrouded in mystery and fear.

Well women, your fear, confidence and confusion are about to pack their bags and head off into the sunset because I'm going to take you by the hand and show you **EXACTLY** how to achieve any goal. That's right – **ANY GOAL**!

You see, goal achievement is very much a process of moving from one place to another, just like the above maze concept described. If you don't know the route that leads to your destination, you'll just keep wandering around in circles.

Ah, but what if someone gave you a map, a step-by-step guide that told you exactly where to turn, which route to take, and led you easily to the end of the maze? I bet you'd have no trouble succeeding then! In fact you would be able to confidently manifest your dream business and life effortlessly.

The problem is that a map written by someone else can only help you so much. Unless the creator of the map lives inside your head and knows your unique position in life, your skills, your strengths, your weaknesses - any guide they provide will be vague and general; untargeted to what YOU want to accomplish.

There is a solution, however. What if you could write your OWN map? What if you had a guide that could take you through a simple, step-by-step process that reveals the most focused action steps, how to prepare for dealing with obstacles, how to objectively evaluate your progress and change direction when necessary as you go along?

This **Step-by-Step Easy to Implement Guide** can give you that, and more. Come along with me as I guide you in developing your own focused, targeted, personalized map – a map that will lead you wherever you choose to go!

Are you ready? Let's begin.

Step One: Specify the Goal

In order to achieve any goal, you have to first know **exactly** what you're trying to achieve, and you must be SPECIFIC!

Most of us make the mistake of being vague with our goals. We say things like:

I want to lose weight. I want more money.

I want a better job. I want to be happy.

That's like going into a restaurant and telling the waitress, "I want something to eat."

You'll need to be a LOT more specific when you set your goals. Each goal you set should include this information:

❖   What

❖   Where

❖   How

❖   Whom (if others are involved or affected)

❖   When

❖   Why

Here is brief explanation of each point:

What: this should identify the "meat" of your goal. What you want to accomplish.

Where: location, if applicable (like getting a job in your local area or moving to a new area).

How: you may have a preference as to "how" events will unfold (this may not always be within your control, but having a general expectation is good).

Whom: if your goals involve others, you'll want to highlight your expectations.

When: a general timeline for the fulfillment of your goals.

Why: your reasons for wanting to achieve your goals. Be very specific on these reasons and try to focus on the BENEFITS (the positive gains), not just the avoidance of what you DON'T want. Instead of saying, "I don't want to be broke anymore" you should word it more positively: "I want to have an abundant flow of money."

WARNING: Do NOT proceed with the rest of the steps unless you are very clear about what you want to accomplish. Clarity is vital! A vague idea will not cut it; you'll just end up wasting your time. Not only will you be confused about how to accomplish such a vague goal, you also won't be able to generate the level of motivation and tenacity needed to see it through.

If you're having trouble figuring out what you want, take the time to find out.

Think about every area of your life, your business and ask yourself what you would change if you could. What would you ADD to your life, your business and what would you TAKE AWAY? This line of thought will lead you in the right direction for creating better circumstances.

Once you are crystal clear about what you want to accomplish, put it into a neat, concise statement:

❖   I want to achieve _____[what]

❖   at _____ [where]

❖   by _____ [how]

❖   by _____ [timeline]

❖   with _____ [other persons]

❖   because _____ [why].

That looks a little confusing with all the blanks; let's use a couple of examples:

I want to start an ecommerce business earning $100,000 per year in my city of Summerville by December 28, 2015, by showing my potential and drive to my mentor(s) and convincing them I am ready to take the necessary action steps to get the job done. I want this business because I am passionate about shopping and I know I would enjoy a business in ecommerce, while earning an extraordinary income and providing for my family.

Here's another:

I want to lose 100 pounds by reducing my consumption of junk food, eating more fruit and veggies, detoxing, taking nutritional vitamins and starting a simple workout routine that is easy to stick with. I want to lose an average of 5 pounds per week for approximately 12 weeks. I want to do this because I will gain a better quality of life, increased energy and a sense of pride about my body.

Notice that these examples are very DETAILED; follow the same format and write your statement here:

_____

_____

_____

_____

Step Two: Breaking It Down

Every large goal is comprised of smaller parts. Sometimes these smaller parts are different facets of a bigger goal, and sometimes they are simply identical, measured increments of the big goal.

Here's what I mean:

A goal like earning a master degree in ecommerce will have many different facets that make up the final goal, such as researching and applying to specific ecommerce degree programs, taking and completing the required credit courses in the ecommerce field, completing a research project or thesis, and finally graduation. These activities are all components of the larger goal.

A goal of losing 100 pounds will involve setting clear action steps such as eating less junk food, eating more veggies and fruit, detoxing, taking nutritional vitamins, exercising regularly – and simply repeating these SAME steps over and over until you reach your goal weight.

There are exceptions of course, depending on the specifics of your goal. How many parts each goal has will vary widely depending on the goal itself, as well as the amount of legwork and preparation you have already done.

However, aim for a minimum of 5 smaller parts of your goal. If you can think of more, go ahead and add them. Start with at least five, and be as detailed as you can.

Step Three: Identify Clear Action Steps

Now that you've specified your goal and broken it down into smaller components, it's time to think about the action steps that will move you toward the finish line.

Give your goal some thought, and consider which key activities would create the results you desire. Your answers will depend on the specifics of your goal, the type of goal, and what you need to do to get there.

There are typically two types of action steps. The first kind pertains to planning and preparation. This would include activities like research and education – laying the groundwork for the bigger action steps you'll take later. Obviously, if you haven't done this part yet your focus should be on this type of activity.

A word of warning: don't let yourself get stuck in the planning and preparation stage! You may feel inclined to do more and more and more research because you don't feel "ready" to take bolder action. Some people get stuck in this phase for years. Eventually you will have to believe that you've researched and planned enough and it's time to move forward. You will HAVE to move forward if you want to succeed.

If you've already laid the groundwork, it's important to focus on PRODUCTIVE actions; the actions that will carry the most power, the actions that will inspire the greatest results.

Additionally, you should identify action steps to be taken daily, weekly, and monthly.

Remember, goal achievement is a **process** – you can't take action just once and hope it works. Most goals will require consistent effort, specific action steps taken day after day, week after week, month after month! Identify the things you can do on a regular basis to keep your plans moving forward.

Daily actions are usually small to moderate in scale but hold the power of duplication and accumulation. The more you do them, the more effective they become.

Weekly actions are usually a bit larger in scale, take a little longer to complete, and involve an element of risk. They are usually the most proactive in the sense that they help you face your fears and push forward determinedly. They would include things like releasing your creations to the public, or increasing your business marketing efforts by attracting attention to your products or services. These bolder actions usually bring about bigger results.

Monthly actions are things you do to keep yourself on track, like evaluate your progress and readjust your plans if necessary. Monthly actions can also include extraneous activities not vital to your goal except in peripheral ways. This can include networking, expanding your market reach, working on your personal development, reading, learning, researching, etc.

Below, list the most productive actions you can determine should be done daily, weekly and monthly. It's important to note that you are not setting a schedule with this exercise; you are simply identifying key, productive action steps that you can take on a daily, weekly and monthly basis. Don't get caught up wondering how you can find time to do all this, or whether a certain task should be done daily or weekly. Simply put down a **general** idea of the most productive actions that you can think of. You can always add to this list or change it later on.

Daily Action Steps

These should be on the smaller side, easily attainable yet effective and focused:

Weekly Action Steps

These should be larger steps that involve an element of risk or aggressive forward movement:

Monthly Action Steps

These should be extraneous steps like evaluating your progress, networking, etc.:

Step Four: Set a General Timeline for Completion

This part of the process has the potential to fuel your efforts, or stall them completely.

On one hand, setting a deadline can be incredibly motivating. It can urge you to stay focused, push yourself to work harder and smarter, and be proactive in overcoming obstacles.

On the other hand, a deadline can cause immense impatience and frustration if things don't move along at the pace you expect.

Read the last word in the sentence above again: EXPECT.

Our expectations get us into trouble more often than we'd like to admit. If we expect something to go well and it doesn't, we feel angry and disappointed. If we expect results by a certain date and it doesn't happen due to circumstances beyond our control, we can lose all hope and give up because it seems worthless to continue. I'm sure you've experienced situations like these before

– most of us have.

While it's favorable to set a GENERAL TIMELINE for completion of your goal, you would be wise to DETACH EMOTIONALLY from any firm expectations.

What do I mean by "detach emotionally"? I mean don't get **hooked** on the idea of certain things happening at a certain time – especially if those "things" are largely out of your control.

Instead, focus more on your actions than the results. Set a timeline for completion of each of your ACTION STEPS, rather than the results you see from your action steps.

Also, be sure not to set unrealistic timelines. Don't create more stress for yourself by taking on a massive project and expecting to complete it within a few days. Moderate, consistent actions will be more effective than getting burned out.

List your key action steps below, with an estimation of the time needed to complete them:

Now set a **GENERAL TIMELINE** for completion of your ultimate goal:

Step Five: Plan B

If you've ever come to a screeching halt with a goal because you encountered a big obstacle, you know the importance of having an alternate plan. As much as we'd like to hope that things will always go according to plan, we know better.

Having a "Plan B" for every step of your journey can save you a lot of time, not to mention frustration! Imagine the difference between feeling immobilized because your path is blocked, or calmly switching gears and moving to Plan B. It can make or break the fulfillment of your goals.

It's easy to forget that there are numerous paths leading to any desired outcome. While we might be attracted to one path over another, ultimately the outcome is the most important thing, right?

In order to ensure stable momentum, take a few minutes to prepare an alternate plan for each part of your goal. Focus not only on alternate paths to the final goal, but alternate activities for each of your action steps.

Here is a simple way to identify viable alternate activities: as you review each step, consider the question, "What would I do if this step or activity was not possible?"

Examples:

If I didn't get accepted into the ecommerce degree program, I could: enroll in non-credit courses to expand my knowledge of the topic, seek an entry-level position to prepare myself for my business experience at a related organization, or explore volunteer opportunities at related organizations.

If my weight loss stalls for more than 4 weeks, I could: increase the intensity of my workouts, eliminate refined foods from my diet, or increase my water consumption.

List your key action steps and activities below and identify some alternate plans:

Step Six: The Right Mind-Set for Success

By now you should have a clear, detailed plan for achieving your goal. You should know exactly what you want, have a solid idea of the smaller components that make up your larger goal, have a list of specific action steps to take, and a general expectation about both the completion of your activities and the culmination of your goal. You've even done your homework and formed alternate plans so you won't get sidetracked if something goes wrong.

How could you fail with a plan like this? You couldn't . . . unless your own thoughts begin to work against you.

There are three key things to keep in mind if you want to stay focused and motivated. Commit to your goal.

You must be willing to keep working toward what you want no matter how difficult it may seem at times. You must be willing to ignore your inner critic (or actual criticism from people in your life) and push on in spite of any negative comments. You must make a strong promise to yourself that you will NOT give up, no matter what obstacles you encounter.

You must make the achievement of your goal the most important thing in your life. Without this level of commitment, you will find it very easy to slack off, get distracted, or give up altogether.

Take action!

The most detailed and effective plan is worthless if you never put it into action. Make a promise to yourself that you will take action immediately and consistently, despite any feelings of fear or hesitation.

Remember that your results are dependent upon the intensity and frequency of your actions. If you want big results, take big actions. If you don't mind smaller results while you're building up your confidence, then start with smaller actions, but ACT.

Let go.

Don't get caught up in frustration about things you can't control. Don't worry about seeing results right away. Don't try to force things to happen in response to your efforts - just focus on taking action, following your plan and keeping your eyes on the prize.

Focus more on enhancing your own performance, stretching your limits and refining your approach. Detach from unrealistic expectations and instead keep your attention directly on what you CAN control, which is your own actions.

Step Seven: Evaluate Your Progress

You might think that evaluation is pointless because you'll either see results or you won't. Not necessarily! Remember that goal achievement is a process and nothing is carved in stone.

Sometimes you'll notice small results, but not as much as you'd like so you need to tweak your plans slightly to adjust the outcome. You'll figure out that changing your approach on one simple thing will explode your results like crazy!

Evaluation is a worthwhile activity because it can help keep you honest about your efforts, it can reveal holes in your plans and it can inspire you to keep going when you notice even moderate results happening.

There are two types of evaluation you should do periodically. The first involves frequent evaluation of your daily actions.

Every one to two weeks, take a few moments to answer these questions:

❖ Are you sticking to your original plans?

❖ Could you improve upon your actions in any way?

❖ Have you had to move to Plan B at any time?

❖ If so, how did that work out for you?

❖ Can you see room for improvement in your original plans?

❖ Have you made any modifications?

❖ If so, are they working better for you?

❖ Have your results met your expectations so far?

❖ If not, why not?

❖ What can you do to improve your results?

The other type of evaluation can be done monthly or even quarterly; and it should focus more on your long-term progress rather than your daily actions.

Answer these questions:

❖ Are your plans moving you in the right direction?

❖ Is your ultimate goal still the same, or are you considering a change in direction?

❖ Can you think of any ways to improve upon your original plans?

❖ What are you learning about yourself through this process?

❖ Have you developed a stronger appreciation of any aspect of yourself?

❖ Which of your qualities and habits still need improvement?

❖ How can you begin to expand your potential and stretch your limits?

❖ Are you beginning to think of even larger goals you can achieve now?

Step Eight: Repeat, Repeat, Repeat!

Do you see now that every goal has a clearly defined route leading to its manifestation? Do you see how with a fair amount of planning and foresight, you can easily achieve any objective?

No matter what goals you set now or in the future, you have an easy-to-duplicate formula that will help you achieve them. Let's recap the steps:

- ❖   Specify the goal.

- ❖   Break it down into smaller parts.

- ❖   Set clear action steps.

- ❖   Set a general timeline for completion.

- ❖   Form a "Plan B" for each action step.

- ❖   Train your mind to commit, take action, and let go.

- ❖   Evaluate your progress frequently.

- ❖   Repeat, repeat, repeat.

Once you become comfortable with these steps, goal achievement will become a simple and pleasant experience for you – no matter WHAT you want to attain.

You'll know how to conquer your inner demons (like fear and confusion), face challenges head- on, and move quickly and precisely to your chosen outcome.

Through the process of choosing your own outcomes and making it your mission to achieve them, you will strengthen and empower yourself more than you would believe is possible.

You'll realize that your quality of life is completely within your control, and you need to only follow a specific route to reach any destination you desire.

Then simply repeat the process to get to your next destination, and the next, and the next!

It's as easy as lacing up your walking shoes and taking a stroll around the neighborhood. You may encounter some hills and valleys, perhaps a bit of smog or an aggressive dog or two, but just keep walking and you'll get where you want to go.

You have the keys to manifest your dream business and life right at your fingertips. See you at the top beautiful!!

Let your beautiful light shine from within and empower other women to do the same.

-Charlotte Howard

How Will You Confidently Follow Your Dreams Today?

How Will You Confidently Follow Your Dreams Today?

Daija Howard

Daija Howard, the chief executive editor at Heart Centered Women Publishing and chief executive coordinator for Beaut Lifestyle Women Retreats.

She is the youngest women's life mentor who has edited and contributed to helping over 40 books become international best sellers.

Learn more at:

http://www.HeartCenteredWomenPublishing.com
http://www.TheHairArtistAssociation.org
http://facebook.com/daijahoward

Positive Thinking for Extraordinary Results

I'm sure you have a bright idea hidden somewhere in the back of your mind that you just can't wait to test out. Of course you're not the only one with the bright idea. So what motivates you to churn those creative or even inspiring juices to its utmost flavor?

It's always best to set up a personal goal where you can accomplish the most in record time, maybe like mowing the lawn in an hour before the big game on TV. A correct and positive attitude in whatever you do will make things easier, and even enjoyable.

Here are some tips to make it through the week even if you're just sitting on your favorite couch. An idea takes time to form in your head and is always at work while you are busy sitting, sleeping, or doing other tasks.

Having a bit of positive thinking can help you realize things that you never thought were possible. Try to see the positive even in the most worst situations. Thinking big is indeed the American Way and that is what made our country prosperous.

1.   Take passionate action towards living your life by design. Talk is cheap. Action = deposits in the bank of a passionately authentic future. Without it passion is void. Feed the passion, nurture your mind.

This is a perfect example where dreams are made of where you start by tinkering with your mind, then with your hands. If the idea weakens, you can always go back to it later until you finish it.

2.   Commit to yourself as well as those you love to create a powerful a life you can love and adore. Instead of reacting,

commit to creating from your heart and soul, out of love rather than fear. The American Dream will always be there, but a dream will still be a dream without motion. Be amazed as the transformation begins.

3.   Recognize and embrace the thought that each moment is perfect regardless of its outcome. Every time you hit on something that may appear too extreme, why not give it a shot and see if it will work. You will be surprised to see if there are other ways to get the task done in time. If you are not pleased with the outcome, decide to use that moment to learn from and make the appropriate shift.

4.   Dwell completely in a place of gratitude. Learn to utilize what you have in your hands and make use of it in the most constructive way. Slipping into neediness will become less of a habit when you repeatedly shift towards gratitude, away from poverty consciousness.

5.   Use a Passion Formula of Recognize/Reevaluate/Restore in place of the Shoulda/Woulda/Coulda whirlwind. The former is based in increased knowledge and abundance while the latter focuses on scarcity and lack. As you face people or tasks that may seem harder than scaling the summit of the Himalayas, allow yourself to realize that the task is just as important as giving out orders to your subordinates. You would rather be richly passionate!

6.   Keep humor at the forefront of thought, laughing at and with you when possible. You may find yourself quite entertaining when you loosen up! I am yet to see a comedian ever go hungry even though his jokes are as 'old as great-grandma'. Life has so much to offer to allow you to mope around in self- pity. Humor is very attractive, very passionate: life-giving.

7.   Believe that you are the architect of your destiny. No one can take your passionate future from you except for you! Create

your life authentically. As long as there's still breath in your body, there is no end to how much you can accomplish in a lifetime. The concept of thinking big is all about enjoying your work, which would lead to celebrate a discovery that is born within your hands. Watch everything flow into place with perfect, passionate precision.

It's interesting how people get caught up by something trivial as learning to use a computer, when nowadays the top computer companies are manufacturing software that even my three year old brother can do it. I don't mean to be condescending, but that's the idea of not having any positive thinking in your life-you'll just end up as a dim bulb in a dark corner. So instead

of subjecting yourself to what you will be doomed for, make your path by taking the first step with a positive attitude.

Enthusiasm is what makes the difference between reaching our goals and giving up before we get started. Thomas Edison said, "If the only thing we leave our kids is the quality of enthusiasm, we will have given them an estate of incalculable value." Edison's research laboratory burned to the ground when he was 67. As the fire consumed his world-famous "invention factory," Edison told his children, "Kids, go get your mother. She'll never see another fire like this one." Edison knew that enthusiasm is the best antidote for tragedy, and it's the most powerful weapon to use in the war against procrastination.

I have learned that my level of enthusiasm has nothing to do with my feelings; my feelings wake up on a different side of the bed every day. To take control of my life, I must choose the way I feel-I can't let my feelings control me.

Success is not handed to you on a silver platter. It takes time, effort and dedication to achieve success. Your Passion for what you love to do will fuel your desire to work during the tough times, and will help you create success on a whole new level. Create your own reality using your god given talents.

We must continue to learn new things as if we were going to live forever, while living each day as if it were the last. Telling myself that "Today is the first day of the rest of my life" doesn't work for me. If today were the last day of my life, how would I live it? That is the question I ask myself when I fight against the forces of procrastination.

Always remember that enthusiasm is a choice. Mark Twain said, "Do something every day that you don't want to do; this is the golden rule for acquiring the habit of doing your duty without pain."

As a woman it is very important to conquer your challenges. They help you improve your personal and professional life with ease.

Does any of this sound familiar to you?

- Your plate is full.

- Overflowing in fact.

- On any given weekend or late evening, chances are you can be found helping others.

Have you thought about delegating? Most of us have.

Delegating enables us to have better work and life balance, to develop others, encourages teamwork, provides a richer array of perspectives on any given project, and, utilizes everyone's skills and talents more efficiently.

So, let's take a look at the reasons why so often we tend not to ask others to contribute in delivering the work we do.

• It won't get done, or it won't get done correctly

• I'll just have to nag until it gets done

• They are really busy too

- I don't have help

- No one else can do it

- I want to be recognized for my contributions

These are all perfectly good reasons for not wanting to delegate but in this instance, you can "have your cake and eat it too!"

Do you want a healthy personal and professional lifestyle? Do you want your life back?

You can delegate, and the work will get done and, here's the kicker-you will be a better woman for it! Does this sound familiar?

If you couldn't fail, what would you do?

Many women don't do things because they are afraid to fail or they have failed in the past. If there is something that you would do for sure if you knew there isn't a chance whatsoever of failing at achieving your goal what would that be?

If you were forced to start over again, what would you do?

Many women find themselves in situations where they are not doing as they wish they were. They go to work because they have to, not enjoying a single day of it. If you started over again would you take advantage of the new beginning or would you go back to where you are? What would you do?

If money wasn't an issue, what would you do?

Many women have dreams they wish to confidently follow but they never attempt to move forward with the dreams because they cannot afford to get started. Think of what you would love to do if you had the money to do it. This can be anything.

What is your biggest dream?

If you have a big dream, what is it? There must be something you really want that you dream about. Think about this one thing and focus on it.

What is the biggest barrier stopping you from confidently following your dream?

Name all of the things that have caused you to not follow your big dreams. These things could be people who do not support you, money, fears, and other things. There are many different types of barriers which can be overcome. You might not see opportunity or success with your dreams. You might not even be skilled and lack talent. These could be barriers causing you not to move forward.

What passion are you afraid of owning or admitting?

Many women have dreams and passions of being in business for themselves but they are afraid to talk about it out of fear of being made fun of by other people. You might think your passion is silly to other people. What is this one thing?

As a child, what did you really want to be?

Did you have dreams of becoming an entrepreneurial woman as a child and it didn't turn out quite as expected? Do you still wonder what it would have been like if you did follow your dreams as a child? If you had the opportunity, would you follow this dream today?

If you were going to die in the near future, what would you regret not doing?

Many women have regrets when they realize they are going to die real soon. It is often too late for many women to go back and change the things they missed out on. They would have lived their lives completely differently if they had the chance. If a doctor told you that you hadn't any time left but a few weeks, then what would your regrets be? What would you want to do before your time was up?

Now that you have answered these questions you should have a good idea of your dream path. Knowing these things is very important. It will help you to shape the passion driven lifestyle and business you desire.

Your passion comes from inside and if you truly love what you are doing then this will come naturally for you. You will take pride in your work and if you design hats then you won't send a low quality hat out to a customer because you will be passionate about the quality. This is because you will own it and your name will be on it.

There are endless opportunities waiting for you right now. All you have to do is go and pick them up. No matter what you do in your life, you can always make a difference and leave a legacy behind. No passion driven idea or work is small enough to be unimportant. Everyone has the potential to leave a long lasting footprint in this world. Recognizing this is what enables many women to persist even in the face of challenges.

Success only comes to those who are passionate about fulfilling their dreams while keeping positive thoughts, focusing on the good aspects of their lives and the lives of others and are always ready to face their challenges head on. It's simple to confidently follow your dreams when you adopt these principles.

Can you talk yourself into a positive frame of mind when you're dream stealers have discouraged you? How do you keep yourself motivated? How do you stay focused when a job is tedious? How do you handle failure when your plan isn't going well?

• Stay away from negative people. Attitudes are contagious- negative people infect us with negative attitudes. Associate with positive thinkers; their self-confidence is contagious, too.

• Schedule difficult tasks for the time of day when your energy is highest. If you haven't determined the best time for you to tackle the day's least appealing jobs, try doing them as early as possible.

- Tackle a problem that's been a thorn in your side. When you get in the habit of making things happen, your enthusiasm goes through the roof. Inactivity is a major cause of depression and anxiety. (On the other hand, you can increase your energy level without eliminating other forces that cause procrastination; teenagers are particularly adept at expending enormous amounts of energy without getting anything done. Always remember that any technique is only effective when used as part of a total strategy.)

It makes no difference how many mountains you climb if there is no pleasure. —Charlotte

How Will You Confidently Follow Your Dreams Today?

How Will You Confidently Follow Your Dreams Today?

Sharon Nicholas

Sharon Nicholas is a wife, mother, author, women's mentor, global thought leader with a classic American core beliefs. Nicholas today inspires and motivates women around the world. Inspiring women not only to live their lives authentically, but to live healthier while being becoming who they were destined to be.

Learn more at:

http://www.sharonnicholas.com
https://twitter.com/sharonnicholas http://thinyouwantsout.com
http://heartcenteredwomenmedia.com

Becoming An Overcomer

I've endured many difficulties in my life. I am a product of a struggle, constant determination and perseverance over the odds. Many life events have formed me into the person I am today. To look at my life today, the outsider looking in may not recognize my history or the struggles I've had. They would never know the story of my life and the hard fought journey I've had.

We all have a journey; some journeys are easier than others. My path has always not been easy. Growing up the eldest of three children in a middle class and city environment, it was not a silver spoon life. My life has had many challenges and many rewards. One thing I do know if I had a different mindset my life would have been completely different today. I do know that for a fact.

Really when it comes down to it, there are two types of mindsets in this world. Those who accept their life's circumstance and the environment they're born into. Then there are those who don't. Some purposely force their lives to improve with vision, determination and inner strength. They clearly make the decision and seek out change. Others settle into to life and don't question or desire for more in life. Some live out their years and in the struggle, but in reality they don't have to settle. Many times it's a choice which was made. It's truly a decision some make. They've made along the way to accept difficult circumstances.

Some of us are natural born fighters who question everything. Who continually are challenging the status quo and strive for personal growth and improvement. Those of us who are up for the challenge make the decision and welcome change. Some are truly born as prizefighters in life; born to overcome any challenge. Fewer people seize ownership of their own life and personal destiny. We know many people once they make the decision to change they will truly thrive. So why does is seem more don't make the decision for personal change than make the choice?

Adversity fuels fire in some, empowers creative thinking and out the box solutions. Challenges in life build us stronger to ultimately succeed on a larger scale.

Sometimes the challenge has nothing to do with something we've personally created, it's from birth. The geographic location of where one is born can have a major impact on learning, earning potential, careers and outcome for some, but not all of us. Some of us never let birth circumstances deter us.

For some socioeconomic conditions one's born into cause much of their adversity. From the start some are born with family baggage, even from the day they are born. Some of us are born into less than perfect circumstances, but yet we ourselves are perfect. Perfectly capable of doing anything we set our minds to. A positive mindset is critical to success especially when you are born in a tough place such as an inner city or disadvantaged rural environment facing severe hardships. Even if you come from a loving home you can face many challenges every day.

Getting an education and maintaining a job are both are fairly difficult for many. It can seem nearly impossible to achieve without basic resources. Many have more obstacles to overcome just to survive and provide the necessities of life. Life is full of difficultly, but not impossible to overcome.

When you are born middle class, poverty level or below poverty level it's not as easy to achieve and maintain any sense of normalcy from day to day at times. Maintaining a job with a living wage is more difficult without an education. Being able to pay the bills is more of a challenge. Keeping food on the table is your main concern. Many face daily challenges of survival the rest of the world doesn't ever know. Most of the America has never experienced it, so how would they possible know? To hear of challenges is one thing; to live them is another story. Some of us get up each day and work harder than the previous day. We want more, but not out of greed or envy, but simply because of the God-given drive we're born with. We want our children to be more comfortable then we were at times as children.

With my own life story, it's has had moments of adversity like anyone's journey. Regardless of everything I am optimist and my sense of belief has carried me on. My early years were filled with extreme love while also filled with some dramatic events and obstacles to overcome along the way. Just to get an education to start my own life was a struggle at times. I had already lived a whole lifetime by the age of 25, full of life changing events.

My parents themselves worked hard every day. They were a great example of the hardworking American family. I was raised with classic American ideals. The dream of owning a home and raising a family were the cornerstone of our life. My parents were the most loving parents a child could ask for. My father was a super hard worker. His mission was to build the best life for his family he possibly could. He himself came from a large hardworking family. I can remember my father working a tremendous amount of overtime to give us a better life.

The largest life event in my childhood and really has been the largest defining moment in my life was the passing of my father. Right after my 13th birthday my father died of a massive heart attack. He passed away while were on vacation. He passed away in front of his young family. As traumatic and sad as this event was, our family continued to stay close and succeed through many tough years following his death. My father was such a solid man and formed me into the person I am today. My father and I were extremely close. He forever left his family in gratitude for everything he'd done for us, providing everything he could financially to give us a better life.

He left such a strong impression on me for his dedication to his family and his extreme work ethic, he was well known for. My father really molded me into the person I am today. Through his example, the way his lived his life and commitment to his family inspired me.

My mother was an extremely dedicated and devoted mother with one mission to make sure we all had college educations. She wanted us to all have educations badly, because she herself never went to college. I was the first person in her immediate family to attend college. Even that was not easy by any means. I was always struggling with paying bills, while trying to get an education all while working my way through college. A few scholarships helped and I worked odd jobs to pay for my education along the way. I was the first to graduate in my mother's immediate family.

Sadly, during my college years my mother was diagnosed with late stage breast cancer. She taught me what it was to fight. She fought cancer with the same passion and humor she had throughout her life. My mother had married my father later in life. She had children later in life which we believe was related to her breast cancer years later developing. Through cancer treatment she did survive and lived on for more than a decade after treatment. My mother was a fighter and the rock of our family. She had to be our rock. My mother was a single parent of three young children. My mother had three young children to ages 13, 10 and 9 to care for at the time of my father's passing. She did an amazing job as a single mother.

What I have learned from all of these events in my own life is you must have perseverance at all times and carry that same strength throughout life's events. I have learned to always have goals for your own life; it's vital to your own success and your family's future. I've learned courage is when someone who is not naturally brave musters up the strength to take on adversity as their motivator and thrives.

To live your life fully with courage is what we strive for, to live and be fully present. Some things I've learned to hold true to your vision of your own life and your future goals. I've learned to hold true to what you personally value as important. You must never let anyone stop you or say you can't accomplish your goals. You must vision what you'd like to be doing in the future, even it is seems completely impossible at the time. Life has a way of unfolding and opportunities happen by the grace of God. You must dream big first to achieve any success and always allow yourself to dream! You must always have a vision of your life and dream big regardless if it seems foolish at the time. Don't let difficult circumstances stop you. Don't allow lack of skills; lack of funds or the lack of time stop you from making your vision a reality.

All things are built in time with vision, drive and hard work. Once you start on a path, the flow will start to happen. Once you're on the right path, your future will unfold naturally. Your past doesn't determine your future unless you really let it take hold of you. We all have a future. You decide how you want to spend yours with your own mindset. Ambition is built from having a vision of your own potential and the fire to carry it through.

We each have own innate abilities and we should seek out opportunities to use them. By nature some are going to fight to achieve their goals regardless. Some overcome obstacles with sheer will. When we develop a mindset of abundance, embracing our gifts and developing our talent, then our lives improve. We all have gifts it's a matter of finding them and building upon them. To conquer and master your talents is what's expected of you, that's your mission.

Some of the things I have learned to make your life easier. Learning how to maximize your time well only leads to personal and career success. We have to also learn the art of patience. Learning to wait to strike when the moment is right is an art. The right timing is essential for success.

Knowing when the time is right to pursue your dreams helps you succeed with your goals. The right timing, patience and perseverance are required for achieving all things in life.

Learn when it's time to hold back and when it's time to better prepare yourself. Discern when it's time to act, hone your sense of timing and know when the precise moment to expend energy.

Have the determination to make it happen yet have patience to know when. Be patient and wait for the window to open, when the time is right you will know.

Patience and learning to wait to seize the right moment is something athletes know how to do well. Their careers depend on timing and making adjustments on the fly. We as mothers and women have these same skills naturally. We benefit from learning to time ourselves accordingly. We multitask well as women. We learn to circumvent life's mind fields and adjust our lives accordingly to the changes around us. Some changes we bring on ourselves and some are unforeseen events.

If we learn to expend our energy in the right places and at the exact right time we don't burn ourselves out. Start by thinking out your life. What is your biggest goal or dream? Plan the future, wait for the right moment, but don't be complacently sitting by either. Think of ways which daily you can build your own future. Brainstorm regularly and develop your talents.

One of the keys for success is networking with like-minded people. Surround yourself with people with similar interests, visions and goals. Build yourself into who you want to become. Surround yourself with people you admire both personally and professionally. Educate yourself simply by being in the presence of intelligent people who are willing to share their time. Always take advantage of learning from other talented people, they one of your best assets. It helps to plan out your future by the example of others and take charge of your own life with what you'll observe by being around them.

As women, we have to pace ourselves throughout our children bearing years and during our child rearing years we have larger priorities. It comes down to patience and quietly working on your skills. When the time is right and the offer comes your way, you'll be ready.

My thoughts on success:

Know yourself and what you value.

Don't judge yourself harshly or judge yourself by the lives of others. Embark on a mindset reassessment.

Squash your self-doubts and self-hate. Learn to accept failures.

Follow your real passions.

Winners look at failure as education.

Surround yourself with people with a similar life vision and goals. Optimism and enthusiasm open doors.

Fear destroys futures.

Let go of your pass hurts.

Chosen goals should be your own.

Think out and plan out your options before you leap into your future. Take risks and be willing to challenge yourself out of your comfort zone. Appreciate where you are and where you've been.

Praise your own abilities and always love yourself. Authenticity draws others.

Grant yourself the same compassion you grant others. Talent can be trumped by training.

Prioritize your life's goals.

Find a new reason to be grateful daily.

Success comes from stretching your imagination. Choose not to give into circumstances.

Where there is will, with a beating heart and a bright mind there is always a way to make it happen. Be willing to fight and embrace chances to make a better life. Once you make up your mind you want something, don't let any obstacles prevent you from achieving your dreams.

Dreams fulfilled require vision to develop them and then the strength to follow them through. Let nothing impact your goals or our ability to envision the life you'd like to be living with determination, persistence and hard work to carry it out, the future is yours. To defy the odds, seek out and build new opportunities which may have not existed before it's your mission.

Nurturing your mind, body and soul are essential keys to creating an extraordinary life.

-Charlotte Howard

How Will You Confidently Follow Your Dreams Today?

Sonya Davis

Sonya Davis is an accomplished beauty industry expert, author, speaker and leading image consultant. She trains and "EMPOWERS" families worldwide on how to enhance their lives mentally, physically, spiritually and financially. As an international best selling author, paralegal and spiritual ambassador, she uses her god given talents to help others achieve their goals.

Learn more at: http://beautlifestyle.com http://womenlifementor.com https://twitter.com/sonyandavis

Beauty Bombshell Inside and Out

How many times have you gone to sleep at night, swearing you'll go to the gym in the morning, and then changing your mind just eight hours later because when you get up, you don't feel like exercising?

While this can happen to the best of us, it doesn't mean you should drop the ball altogether when it comes to staying fit. What people need to realize is that staying active and eating right are critical for long-term health and wellness -- and that an ounce of prevention is worth a pound of cure.

The more you know about how your body responds to your lifestyle choices, the better you can customize a nutrition and exercise plan that is right for you. When you eat well, increase your level of physical activity, and exercise at the proper intensity, you are informing your body that you want to burn a substantial amount of fuel. This translates to burning fat more efficiently for energy.

In other words, proper eating habits plus exercise equals fast metabolism, which, in turn gives you more energy throughout the day and allows you to do more physical work with less effort.

The true purpose of exercise is to send a repetitive message to the body asking for improvement in metabolism, strength, aerobic capacity and overall fitness and health. Each time you exercise, your body responds by upgrading its capabilities to burn fat throughout the day and night, Exercise doesn't have to be intense to work for you, but it does need to be consistent.

This is where the magic begins, allowing you to become a beauty bombshell inside and out. I recommend engaging in regular cardiovascular exercise four times per week for 20 to 30 minutes per session, and resistance training four times per week for 20 to 25 minutes per session.

This balanced approach provides a one-two punch, incorporating aerobic exercise to burn fat and deliver more oxygen, and resistance training to increase lean body mass and burn more calories around the block.

Here's a sample exercise program that may work for you:

*   Warm Up -- seven to eight minutes of light aerobic activity intended to increase blood flow and lubricate and warm-up your tendons and joints.

*   Resistance Training -- Train all major muscle groups. One to two sets of each exercise. Rest 45 seconds between sets.

*   Aerobic Exercise -- Pick two favorite activities, they could be jogging, walking, biking or cross-country skiing, whatever fits your lifestyle. Perform 12 to 15 minutes of the first activity and continue with 10 minutes of the second activity. Cool down during the last five minutes.

*   Stretching -- Wrap up your exercise session by stretching, breathing deeply, relaxing and meditating.

When starting an exercise program, it is important to have realistic expectations. Depending on your initial fitness level, you should expect the following changes early on.

*   From one to eight weeks -- Feel better and have more energy.

*   From two to six months -- Lose size and inches while becoming leaner. Clothes begin to fit more loosely. You are gaining muscle and losing fat.

*   After six months -- Start losing weight quite rapidly.

Once you make the commitment to exercise several times a week, don't stop there. You should also change your diet and or eating habits. I suggest these easy-to-follow guidelines:

*Detox daily with two cups of iaso tea, this will remove toxins from your body and aid to help with weight loss journey

* Eat several small meals (optimally four) and a couple of small snacks throughout the day

* Make sure every meal is balanced -- incorporate palm-sized proteins like lean meats, fish, egg whites and dairy products, fist-sized portions of complex carbohydrates like whole-wheat bread and pasta, wild rice, multigrain cereal and potatoes, and fist-sized portions of vegetable and fruits

* Limit your fat intake to only what's necessary for adequate flavor

* Drink at least eight 8-oz. glasses of water throughout the day

* I also recommend that you take a liquid multivitamin each day like nutriburst to ensure you are getting all the vitamins and minerals your body needs.

I see everyday women fighting against self-esteem, obesity is a big contributor. There are many ways to lose your sense of self-esteem despite of how trivial it could get. But whatever happens, we should all try not to lose our own sense of self.

So what does it take to be a cut above the rest? Here are some of the things you can think and improve on that should be enough for a week.

Know your purpose

Are you wandering through life with little direction - hoping that you'll find happiness, health and prosperity? Identify your life purpose or mission statement and you will have your own unique compass that will lead you to your truth every time.

This may seem tricky at first when you see yourself in a tight situation. But there's always that little loophole to turn things around and you can make a big difference in yourself.

Know your values

What do you value most? Make a list of your top 5 values. Some examples are security, freedom, family, spiritual development, learning. As you set your goals for this year - check your goals against your values. If the goal doesn't align with any of your top five values - you may want to reconsider it or revise it.

The number shouldn't discourage you; instead it should motivate you to do more than you ever dreamed of.

Know your needs

Unmet needs can keep you from living authentically. Take care of yourself. Do you have a need to be acknowledged, to be right, to be in control, to be loved? There are so many women who lived their lives without realizing their dreams and most of them end up being stressed or even depressed for that matter. List your top four needs and get them met before it's too late!

Know your passions

You know who you are and what you truly enjoy in life. Obstacles like doubt and lack of enthusiasm will only hinder you, but will not derail your chance to become the person you ought to be. Express yourself and honor the people who have inspired you to become the very person you wanted to be.

Live from the inside out

Increase your awareness of your inner wisdom by regularly reflecting in silence. Indulge with nature. Breathe deeply to quiet your distracted mind. For most women it's hard to even find the peace and quiet we want even in our own home. In my case I often just sit in a dimly lit room and play some relaxing music. There's sound, yes, but music does soothe the soul.

Honor your strengths

What are your positive traits? What special talents do you have? List three - if you get stuck, ask those closest to you to help identify these. Are you imaginative, witty, good with your hands?

Find ways to express your authentic self through your strengths. You can increase your self- confidence when you can share what you know to others.

Serve others

When you live authentically, you may find that you develop an interconnected sense of being. When you are true to who you are, living your purpose and giving of your talents to the world around you, you give back in service what you came to share with others -your spirit - your essence. The rewards for sharing your gift with those close to you is indeed rewarding, much more if it were to be the eyes of a stranger who can appreciate what you have done for them.

Self-improvement is indeed one type of work that is worth it. The difference lies within ourselves and how much we want to change for the better. Your keys to success have a vision of who you are and want to be.

Beauty Bombshell Life Mapping: A Vision of Success Inside and Out

Success is more than economic gains, titles, and degrees. Planning for success is about mapping out all the aspects of your life. Similar to a map, you need to define the following details: origin, destination, vehicle, backpack, landmarks, and route.

Origin: Who you are

A map has a starting point. Your origin is who you are right now. Most young women when asked to introduce themselves would say, "Hi, I'm Sarah and I am a 23-year old, college student." It does not tell you about who Sarah is; it only tells you her present preoccupation. To gain insights about yourself, you need to look

91

closely at your beliefs, values, and principles aside from your economic, professional, cultural, and civil status. Moreover, you can also reflect on your experiences to give you insights on your good and not-so-good traits, skills, knowledge, strengths, and weaknesses. Upon introspection, Sarah realized that she was highly motivated, generous, service-oriented, but impatient. Her inclination was in the biological-medical field.

Furthermore, she believed that life must serve a purpose, and that wars were destructive to human dignity.

Destination: A vision of who you want to be

"Who do want to be?" this is your vision. Now it is important that you know yourself so that you would have a clearer idea of who you want to be; and the things you want to change whether they are attitudes, habits, or points of view. If you hardly know yourself, then your vision and targets for the future would also be unclear. Your destination should cover all the aspects of your being: the physical, emotional, intellectual, and spiritual. Continuing Sarah's story, after she defined her beliefs, values, and principles in life, she decided that she wanted to have a life dedicated in serving her country.

Vehicle: Your Mission

A vehicle is the means by which you can reach your destination. It can be analogized to your mission or vocation in life. To a great extent, your mission would depend on what you know about yourself. Based on Sarah's self-assessment, she decided that she was suited to become a doctor in military, and that she wanted to become one. Her chosen vocation was a military medical doctor. Her vision-mission fully: it was to live a life dedicated to serving her country as a doctor.

Travel Bag: Your knowledge, skills, and attitude

Food, drinks, medicines, and other traveling necessities are contained in a bag. Applying this concept to your life map, you also bring with you certain knowledge, skills, and attitudes. These determine your competence and help you in attaining your vision. Given such, there is a need for you to assess what knowledge, skills, and attitudes you have at present and what you need to gain along the way. This two-fold assessment will give you insights on your landmarks or measures of success. Sarah realized that she needed to gain professional knowledge and skills on medicine so that she could become a military doctor. She knew that she was a bit impatient with people so she realized that this was something she wanted to change.

Landmarks and Route: S.M.A.R.T. objectives

Landmarks confirm if you are on the right track while the route determines the travel time. Thus, in planning out your life, you also need to have landmarks and a route. These landmarks are your measures of success. These measures must be specific, measurable, attainable, realistic, and time bound. Thus you cannot set two major landmarks such as earning a master's degree and a doctorate degree within a period of three years, since the minimum number of years to complete a master's degree is two years. Going back to Sarah as an example, she identified the following landmarks in her life map: completing a bachelor's degree in biology by the age of 25; completing medicine by the age of 28; earning her specialization in infectious diseases by the age of 31; getting deployed in local public hospitals of where uncle sam sends her by the age of 33; and serving as doctor in war-torn areas by the age of 35.

Anticipate Turns, Detours, and Potholes

The purpose of your life map is to minimize hasty and spur-of-the-moment decisions that can make you lose your way. But oftentimes our plans are modified along the way due to some inconveniences, delays, and other situations beyond our control. Like in any path, there are turns, detours, and potholes but; we must anticipate them and adjust accordingly.

Enjoy life, we all deserve it.

I would like to thank the women who've brought me through those tough times, when I felt horrible, and betrayed. These lessons have been my greatest teachers of all time. -Charlotte Howard

How Will You Confidently Follow Your Dreams Today?

_____
_____
_____
_____
_____
_____
_____
_____
_____
_____
_____
_____
_____
_____
_____
_____
_____
_____
_____
_____
_____
_____

How Will You Confidently Follow Your Dreams Today?

Theresa Broadnax

Theresa Broadnax is an Emmy Award winning Hair Stylist and Fashion Stylist in Hollywood. Theresa is Founder, Creative Director and Designer of House of Broadnax a Handbag and Leather Goods Company.

Also the visionary voice behind House of Broadnax blog, where she shares fashion tips on dressing like a million without spending a million.

Learn more at:

http://theresabroadnax.com

Mirrored Muse...."The State of Self Reflection"

She who is clothed in confidence has the power to succeed. It starts with the muse in the mirror, one's self reflection. How one sees their self, first you must believe in you. You must be your number one fan, even when others doubt your abilities. Fulfilling ones dreams begins with putting the work in to achieve your goals, success doesn't come to you, you must go to it. Start with asking the person in the mirror, the Mirrored Muse are you doing what is needed to fulfill your dreams.

By following your inspiration the universe will lead you in the direction of your dream. Pursuing your dream is a lesson of growth., keep at it and be persistent. Your actions will determine whether you get knock down or rise up and grow. Once you find your passion and understand what your plan is, set goals. Through the years I've always kept a journal. Writing things down and checking my goals off as I accomplished them, that way you can visionally see that you are getting closer to your dream. Understand that the journey to you making your dreams come true may not be a smooth road, but the experiences along the way will be valuable. Having and setting goals will keep you going, when your reach one goal set another. No one becomes successful by just thinking about it, you have to set goals, map out your plan, and then execute that plan. During this process you must make sure to stay focused on a goal. Don't get stuck on trying different variations of the same ideas. Focus on creating an idea you are happy with and that you feel has innovative potential. Believing in your dream will give you the confidence you need to see it through.

I can't emphasize enough how important keeping a journal or sketchbook is. All of your ideas need to be recorded. Writing down your ideas gives you the ability to refer back to them, at a later date. No one can remember them all. It also gives you a library of ideas guide you when you're not feeling very creative.

From time to time take a look back and consider all that you've already accomplished. Remind yourself of these achievements and give yourself a little pat on the back. It will bring some pleasure and continue to motivate you, to remain focused, and keep you moving forward.

Patience is everything. Stay hungry for success is a term I use often when speaking to mentorship programs. Being driven toward achievements and having the mindset of a winner. Don't worry about blending in, it's always best to stand out when it comes to achievements.

Observe your surroundings and detach yourself from anyone who doesn't share the same hunger and whose goals are not the success oriented. Unfortunately as you thrive towards success people who do not have that same mindset and aren't thriving, may bring negative energy. Sad but true. You don't need anyone around who doesn't feed your hunger for success with positive energy.

The people who support your dreams can help along the way, those who question your dreams and your abilities can help to fuel your determination. I always had doubters along the way, so that was always my fuel. Proving them wrong was my content fuel, and it's nothing like riding on a full tank. Charging your environment will have tremendous influences on your actions, energy and mood.

Create a routine. In doing so you have consistency and content action in your every day practice. Having and keeping a schedule allows you to follow your own rules with focus and discipline.

They say knowledge is power, but knowledge is not power. Knowing a concept is only potential value. The execution of that knowledge is where your power lies. Knowing yourself also gives you the tools to stay discipline, motivated and the ability to execute toward your potential. So always nourish your mind, keep learning and stay curious, but be sure to nourish your body as well. Maintaining healthy eating habits, get moving with some form of exercise and form a better sleep routine. You will be surprised, with even making small positive changes in nutrition, exercise and your sleep pattern can make a significant change in your productivity. With all the choices we make let the journey be fueled by passion and hunger, the two are a unstoppable combination.

Life is about fulfilling our calling and becoming more then you ever imagined. You must take the first step, and if you lack self confidence then that should be your first goal. If you do have self confidence, Then direct it toward your chosen goals. Ask yourself what's holding you back from achieving your goals and fulfilling your dreams, the answer is probably you. Look into your inner self.....the Mirrored Muse, and ask what has kept you from pursuing and conquering these goals. Be bold and use the greatness within you, when you chase after your dreams you have to be willing to run and keep running until you are able to achieve your dreams.

When setting goals decide what you want to achieve in your life, then separate what's important from what's irrelevant. It's important to motivate yourself and to continue to build your self confidence based on successful achievements. Whether you have small dreams or huge expectations, setting goals allows us to plan how we move forward through life.

Goals big and small can be stepping stones to a happier life. I know sometimes your ability to maintain momentum to ensure your accomplishments maybe an issue at times.

When you are not motivated, your determination and commitment are tested. Motivation is the energy that drives us to accomplish goals, and is highly necessary in achieving success. When you feel like you've lost your motivation face it head on, confront it and correct it. Use the power within you to rekindle the fire.

Sometimes you must trust in yourself and have faith that you will reach your goals, despite not having a perfectly laid out plan. You can't predict the future but you have to trust in something, whether it's faith or destiny. Trusting yourself is the first step to feeling inspired. Along the way you need balance, there must be pleasure and there must always be seriousness. Take risk and don't be afraid of failure. Failures are lessons and just like little bumps in your road to success. Keep a steady path and don't steer off track due to any bumps in the road.

Motivation is the key factor in one's success. If you have motivation, you can do anything without being forced. When you are passionate about what you're perusing, it makes everything a little smoother. Always do what you feel pleasure in doing and let your wit be the key to gaining success. Don't be ordinary, people always admire uniqueness and it's the best way to attract attention. When something isn't working, you've got to tweak it. Don't keep banging your head against the wall, pivot and try to tackle the problem from a different angle. When it comes to motivation attitude is everything. What's your vision, what is determining your motivating force. Before you begin ask yourself what is your reason to succeed. Why is it important to you, and are you committed to seeing it through. Having a clear mind is a very important factor.

When your mind is full of ideas and strategies, your mind can go in a million different directions. Writing your thoughts down in a journal and visionally seeing what you've done so far, will give you options for moving forward. Break down your goals into a manageable list. Scheduling time into your agenda for specific tasks that will get you to the next level and closer to your end goals. Keeping motivated and interested is directly related to those successfully met goals. Being realistic in your goal setting will set you up for more success then failure.

Start with small tasks at first. As you get more successes accomplished, make your goals more ambitious. If you have trouble getting and staying in creative mode, find a creative nook. Each creative success you have in that location trains your mind to be creative within its boundaries. Finding your creative cycle, when your body is at its most creative, is also an important factor.

I'm an early morning person, so my super creative time is in the morning. But I'm also up late so I can also get a late night creative recharge. Find out when you're at your creative best, and use that time to your advantage.

In short everything you do affects who you are and who you become. Inspiration is a concept from our thoughts about creativity. Let your definition of inspiration be the empowerment you need to explore and create. Knowing yourself, your strengths and weakness are key elements in conquering your goals. Begin the progress of empowerment by expecting no excuses, and holding yourself accountable for putting the work in to fulfilling your dreams.

Staying focus is one of the key elements in conquering your goals to help keep your energy up. Do creative work first. Check off the tasks that require creatively and concentration first, then move on to easier tasks. If you need help humble yourself and ask for help. Learn as much as you can from people who can guide you in the right direction and realize by fulfilling your dreams, it may require a lifestyle change. I say this to say if you haven't accomplished any of your dreams thus far, this will be a must. Don't fear, it may only require some small adjustments.

Self Reflection will help in improving your self confidence, aid you in having a stronger sense of control and increase your passion to push you closer to fulfilling your dreams and goals.

The Mirrored Muse.....The State of Self Reflection. Self awareness is so critical, and plays a very important part in self improvement and will improve your chances of reaching your goals. I've always used self reflection as a way to push myself toward personal inner growth. An inner cleansing of your mental state is what Self Reflection really is.

You have to discover what sparks a charge in you so you can get your shine on. -Charlotte Howard

Tina A. Hobson

2X International Best Selling Author Tina A. Hobson speaks publicly and advocates for women's rights including prevention of drug abuse and domestic violence. Tina believes that her deliverance from alcohol and drugs is the greatest asset she has to offer the world.

Tina is presently the Hostess of I Am A Superwoman Radio, a Licensed Social Worker and CEO of Tina's Glory Hair, LLC. Tina is also an officer with Toastmasters International. Tina believes that with hard work, tenacity but most of all having faith in the Provider of all, All Things Are Possible.

Learn more at:

http://authortinahobson.com
www.blogtalkradio.com/iamasuperwoman2

Your Vision, Your Dream, Your Purpose

Helen Keller once wrote: The only thing worse than being blind is having sight but no vision. When I first read this quote it hit me like a ton of bricks. I reflected back upon the times in my life when I could best describe myself as having physical sight but not a clue as to what I was seeing. I may as well have been blind. I can describe the dark times of my life as being, sightless; having no idea of what my purpose was in life.

Not knowing where I was going and surely not knowing why. I wandered around aimlessly from place to place, person to person, looking, seeking but not finding. I chuckle now as I remember once being told that "when the pupil is ready, the teacher will appear". At first I really didn't understand what was meant by that statement, but as time progressed and life kept slapping me around like a dish rag, I came to understand and believe.

When the teacher appears I must be able to see him. Seeing not just with physical eyes but most importantly with Spiritual eyes. I must be willing and ready to trudge the course of actions set before me. In other words I must surrender. I must surrender my way of thinking, behaving and believing. I had to be able to see beyond what my feeble mind could perceive and go outside of the box of my own reality and look at the truth.

The Bible states in Hebrews 11:1-2 The fundamental fact of existence is that this trust in God, this faith, is the firm foundation under everything that makes life worth living. It's our handle on what we can't see. The act of faith is what distinguished our ancestors, set them above the crowd.

That is what I call Vision. Vision is not spooky but it can be defined as Supernatural. Supernatural is defined as "Of or relating to existence outside the natural world."

It means to me knowing and believing that there is a Power much greater than myself and it is that Power I must depend on to guide me to where I should go. As I see it, with all the seeking, I was not asking. I, in all actuality, was not ready. I was still trying to live my life by my own strength and attempting to do things my own way, but that's not how it works. Later rather than sooner I came to understand the Bible Scripture which states in Matthew 7:7 "Ask and it will be given to you; seek and you will find; knock and the door will be opened to you.

Clearly, I had left out the first and major part of this Scripture, I had not been asking. God, The Teacher, would eventually appear when I was ready and I asked. It took years of pain and suffering by at last, I, the pupil was ready! After many years of drug/alcohol addiction and domestic violence which left me on death's doorstep, I was ready.

In early November of 1989 I began asking, I began praying, I began seeking Spiritual guidance and professional help for a situation that seemed hopeless and I could not with my finite sight see my way out. Up until this time I had no Vision or Purpose. I had plenty of Dreams but that's all they were, dreams. There was no action taking place, there was no defined plan to make my dreams a reality.

I was talking the talk but not walking the walk. My dreams were huge, huge home, big car, humungous bank account, prestigious profession, I was going to be the mover and shaker. I could tell you what I wanted to be, what I wanted to have and what I wanted to do but if you asked me how it was going to happen I couldn't honestly answer you. I had no idea.

It was in a dark room of a mental institution that I gained my Spiritual sight. It was in that dark lonely room that I became ready to live my Purpose. It was there in that dark lonely room that I sincerely and spiritually connected to the Power Source of my being.

I literally saw the light. I was able to see the reason for the years of pain and suffering, it was because I needed to be humbled, not humiliated as I sometimes did to myself, but humbled before God so that He could use me to get the Glory.

I wondered and asked why I had to go through so much pain. God told me it was because I needed to become as a child again. I had to become teachable again as I was as a child. I needed to be bent, molded, and shaped into the person I was intended to be. God wanted me to live my dreams, vision, dreams and purpose and He did whatever He had to to make it happen.

Today, I am walking in and on Purpose. No, I still don't do everything right or in order, but I least I do them. I am no longer just a dreamer. I have plans with a course of action to follow. My goal is to do God's will not mine. I have been given so many blessings just out of obedience. I don't have everything I want, but I surely have everything I need.

My Purpose is to Empower others, especially women who have found themselves in a dark place. Everything God has given me to do is about helping others follow their personal Vision, Dreams and Purpose.

I have a professional Social Work license; I am the Executive Producer/Director and Host of a popular radio talk show, Author, and Entrepreneur, all of which are meant to empower.

What I am most proud of is that I am a Child of God, The only God who has allowed me to be a productive citizen, daughter, mother, grandmother, great-grandmother, sister, aunt and cousin.

I am a woman of Vision, Spiritual Vision. I can see where I want to go, I can see what and how God's plan for me is. 3 John 1:2 Beloved, I pray that in all respects you may prosper and be in good health, just as your soul prospers. Yes, God wants me to prosper and He gives me the tools to do so. I allow Him to position me with the right people, places and things. He gave me the tool of Vision Boards and my ever so useful Blessing Jar.

I use my Vision Board in two ways; one is to thank God in advance for the things that I want and two, to place those things (Spiritual and material) on the board so that I can reflect and pray upon them daily. Habakkuk 2:2 Then the LORD answered me and said, "Record the vision and inscribe *it* on tablets, That the one who reads it may run.

And yes, my dear, cherished Blessing Jar, this is the Spiritual tool I use to give thanks. Each time that I recognize a blessing that I have been given I write it down on a piece of paper, I sign it with a term of endearment and I place it paper in my jar. At the end of the year I open the jar and reflect upon all of the blessings that God has bestowed upon me that particular year.

Nothing is impossible with God as long as you keep your Spiritual eye on Him, He will never steer you wrong. I will close with a few stanzas of a song written by John Newton (1725-1807), former slave trader, who went from disgrace to Amazing Grace. This has been my theme song for over 25 years. Each time that I want to feel sorry for myself, thinking about my past, all I have to do is just hum this song and a sense of gratitude floods my soul.

Amazing grace! How sweet the sound
That saved a wretch like me!
I once was lost, but now am found;
Was blind, but now I see.

'Twas grace that taught my heart to fear,
And grace my fears relieved;
How precious did that grace appear
The hour I first believed.

Through many dangers, toils and snares,
I have already come;
'Tis grace hath brought me safe thus far,
And grace will lead me home.

The Lord has promised good to me,
His Word my hope secures;
He will my Shield and Portion be,
As long as life endures.

Amazing grace! How sweet the sound
That saved a wretch like me!
I once was lost, but now am found;

Was blind, but now I see.

Never downgrade yourself to satisfy someone else. -Charlotte Howard

How Will You Confidently Follow Your Dreams Today?

Heart Centered Women Publishing, is seeking more amazing women to feature in upcoming inspirational books, anthologies and events?

Contact Charlotte Howard at 803-414-2117 or www.HeartCenteredWomenMedia.com to be considered.